Berlin's Christmas Guide 2024 and Beyond

Explore the Best of Berlin's Holiday Lights, Markets, and Cozy Winter Spots

Jack   Morgan

Disclaimer

This guide is intended to provide information and inspiration for exploring Berlin's Christmas season. While we strive for accuracy, details such as dates, locations, and services may change. Readers are encouraged to verify information with relevant sources before planning their visit. The author and publisher assume no responsibility for any losses or inconveniences incurred as a result of using this guide. Enjoy Berlin responsibly and safely.

Table of Contents

Chapter 3: Iconic Holiday Lights and Decorations

-Where to See Berlin's Most Dazzling Displays

-Festive Streets, Squares, and Landmarks

-Photography Hotspots for Holiday Memories

Chapter 4: Cozy Cafés and Winter Treats

-Warm Up with Berlin's Best Hot Drinks

-Traditional Holiday Foods and Where to Find Them

-Unique Seasonal Dishes and Delicacies

Chapter 5: Berlin's Holiday Events and Performances

-Classical Concerts and Opera for the Season

Chapter 8: Berlin's Historic Christmas Sites

-Churches, Cathedrals, and Nativity Scenes

-Holiday Traditions in Berlin's Historic Districts

-Walking Tour Ideas for a Festive Day Out

Chapter 9: Berlin's Christmas for Kids

Family-Friendly Markets and Rides

Where to See Santa and Festive Parades

Top Activities and Events for Little Ones

Chapter 10: Holiday Reflections: Berlin in a New Year Glow

-New Year's Celebrations in Berlin

-Places to Celebrate and Ring in the New Year

-Post-Holiday Relaxation Spots

Final Tips for a Memorable Berlin Christmas

–Staying Safe and Comfortable in Winter

-Making the Most of Your Berlin Holiday Journey

-Words of Farewell and Inspiration

Welcome to Christmas in Berlin

Introduction to Berlin's Holiday Spirit

As the year draws to a close, Berlin transforms into a winter wonderland that captivates locals and travelers alike.

The city's holiday spirit shines through in every corner—from historic streets adorned with shimmering lights to the aroma of roasted almonds and spiced mulled wine wafting through bustling Christmas markets.

Berliners hold a deep appreciation for tradition, yet the city's holiday season also embraces the creative and modern, making it a unique destination for festive celebrations.

Berlin's holiday traditions blend old and new, honoring classic customs while embracing fresh, vibrant holiday experiences. Here, you'll find traditional German markets alongside contemporary holiday events, set against Berlin's famously diverse and resilient spirit.

Whether you're sipping hot cocoa in a cozy cafe, listening to choirs sing at the Kaiser Wilhelm Memorial Church, or simply walking through snowy boulevards, Berlin invites you to feel the warmth and wonder of its holiday season.

The Magic of Berlin's Winter Season

Winter in Berlin brings a beauty that goes beyond the ordinary. The city takes on a magical glow, with historic landmarks blanketed in snow and lively squares lit up in festive displays. Berlin's winter may be chilly, but its vibrant atmosphere keeps spirits warm.

Here, you'll witness the timeless traditions that make Christmas in Germany so special—candles illuminating windows, children singing carols, and families gathering in celebration.

From the enchanting Gendarmenmarkt, with its artisan booths and twinkling lights, to the avant-garde art installations of Berlin's urban neighborhoods, the season reveals many facets of the city's character.

For the traveler, Berlin offers a holiday experience that feels at once nostalgic and alive with discovery, with each district revealing its own charm and holiday delights.

Whether you're here to explore, reflect, or simply revel in the holiday joy, Berlin's winter season promises a journey full of heartwarming memories and cherished traditions.

Chapter 1: Planning Your Trip

When to Visit for the Full Festive Experience

Berlin's festive season officially kicks off in late November and lasts through the beginning of January, offering an ideal timeframe for travelers seeking the ultimate holiday experience.

For those who want to catch Berlin's famous Christmas markets, visiting between late November and December 24th is perfect, as the markets are in full swing, and the city is alive with holiday cheer.

Many markets and light displays start around November 27th and continue until Christmas Eve, creating a bustling, joyful atmosphere throughout December.

For travelers who enjoy the New Year celebrations or prefer a quieter post-holiday experience, visiting in the last week of December or early January has its own charm.

During this time, the city is still beautifully decorated, and you can enjoy Berlin's cozy winter ambiance without the pre-holiday crowds. New Year's Eve in Berlin is a vibrant occasion, featuring events at landmarks like the Brandenburg Gate, making it an unforgettable way to ring in the new year.

Getting Around the City in Winter

Berlin's public transportation system is well-equipped to handle winter conditions, making it easy for travelers to navigate the city even during the colder months.

The U-Bahn (subway) and S-Bahn (above-ground trains) are efficient, heated, and offer convenient access to nearly every neighborhood, including the popular holiday spots and Christmas markets.

Buses and trams are also available and particularly useful for accessing areas not covered by the train lines.

For a more scenic experience, consider walking through Berlin's neighborhoods, as winter brings a certain charm to the city streets. However, be sure to check the weather and dress accordingly, as some paths may be icy.

If you prefer taxis or rideshares, these are readily available and can provide a warmer, door-to-door option, especially for evening excursions. With options ranging from trains to pedestrian-friendly paths, Berlin is easy to explore, even in the heart of winter.

Essential Travel Tips and Packing Guide

Packing wisely for Berlin's winter is key to making the most of your holiday experience. Berlin winters can be quite chilly, with temperatures ranging from 0°C to -5°C (32°F to 23°F) on average, so layering is essential.

Start with thermal base layers, followed by sweaters or fleece, and finish with a warm, waterproof coat to protect against snow or rain. A cozy scarf, insulated gloves, and a hat are must-haves, especially for outdoor market visits and evening strolls.

Comfortable, waterproof boots with good traction are highly recommended, as Berlin's holiday season often means exploring cobblestone streets or lightly snowy paths.

Don't forget essentials like a power adapter (Berlin uses type C and F outlets), travel-sized toiletries, and a reusable water bottle. And of course, keep a small bag handy for souvenirs from the markets! With the right gear, you'll be prepared to embrace all of Berlin's winter magic, no matter the weather.

Chapter 2: Berlin's Best Christmas Markets

Top Markets You Can't Miss

Berlin is renowned for its festive Christmas markets, each offering a unique atmosphere and a delightful array of holiday treats. Among the most popular markets, the Gendarmenmarkt stands out with its stunning backdrop of the French and German Cathedrals.

Here you can find beautifully handcrafted gifts, traditional German foods like bratwurst and potato pancakes, and warm mugs of glühwein (mulled wine) to sip as you wander.

Another must-visit is the **Alexanderplatz Christmas Market,** which is perfect for families. Featuring a gigantic Christmas tree and a nostalgic carousel, this market is lively and fun, with plenty of stalls selling festive snacks and unique gifts.

Don't miss the **Charlottenburg Palace Market**, where the majestic palace creates a romantic setting for visitors to enjoy artisanal crafts, delicious food, and beautiful decorations.

Each of these markets reflects Berlin's diverse culture and spirit, making them unforgettable stops on your holiday journey.

Hidden Gems and Local Favorites

While the larger markets attract many visitors, Berlin is home to several hidden gems that locals adore. The Winterwald (Winter Forest) market in **Görlitzer Park** is a cozy alternative, offering a more intimate atmosphere surrounded by lush greenery.

Here, you'll find handcrafted goods and organic food stalls, along with local musicians performing live music in a relaxed setting.

Another local favorite is the **Sternschnuppenmarkt** in Wilmersdorf, which combines traditional and contemporary holiday elements.
With fewer tourists, this market allows for a more authentic experience where you can

interact with local vendors and discover unique handmade crafts.

Additionally, the Kreuzberg Christmas Market, held in a vibrant multicultural neighborhood, showcases a variety of international cuisines, making it a perfect spot for adventurous eaters looking to try something new alongside classic German fare.

Market Tips for Families, Couples, and Solo Travelers

Navigating Berlin's Christmas markets can be a joyful experience for everyone, but a few tips can help enhance your visit, regardless of your travel style.

For families, arriving early in the day can help you avoid crowds and give kids the chance to explore activities like puppet shows and carousel rides.

Bring a backpack with snacks and extra layers to keep everyone comfortable while enjoying the festive atmosphere.

Couples seeking a romantic experience should consider visiting in the evening when the markets are beautifully lit. Sharing a warm mug of glühwein while strolling hand-in-hand under the twinkling lights creates a magical ambiance.

Look for quieter spots away from the main stalls to find a cozy corner to sit and soak in the atmosphere.

Solo travelers can enjoy the freedom of exploring at their own pace. Consider joining a guided market tour to learn more about the history and traditions behind each market.

Immerse yourself in the local culture by striking up conversations with vendors or other visitors.

Embrace the spirit of exploration, and don't hesitate to try new foods and beverages along the way.

Each market offers a unique slice of Berlin's holiday spirit, making it easy to create lasting memories during your visit.

Chapter 3: Iconic Holiday Lights and Decorations

Where to See Berlin's Most Dazzling Displays

As winter blankets Berlin, the city transforms into a dazzling spectacle of lights, casting a warm glow over its historical landmarks and vibrant neighborhoods.

One of the must-see displays is at **Kurfürstendamm**, Berlin's famous shopping street. Here, the entire boulevard sparkles with thousands of twinkling lights, creating a festive atmosphere that entices both shoppers and sightseers.

Don't miss the magnificent Christmas Tree at the **Kaiser Wilhelm Memorial Church,** adorned with bright ornaments and illuminated in a way that highlights its beautiful architecture.

Another highlight is the **Brandenburg Gate**, where stunning light installations and projections adorn this iconic monument.

Visiting this site at dusk provides the perfect opportunity to witness the interplay of history and modern artistry, as the gate is bathed in colorful hues and festive decorations.

The Potsdamer Platz is also a focal point during the holiday season, with its dazzling light displays and a massive Christmas tree that draws crowds for evening festivities.

Festive Streets, Squares, and Landmarks

Beyond the famous attractions, Berlin's neighborhoods come alive with holiday cheer through enchanting decorations and lively atmospheres.

Friedrichstraße is another notable area, where elegant lights drape over the street, enhancing the charm of its boutique shops and restaurants.

The bustling Alexanderplatz square transforms into a winter paradise, filled with lively markets and stunning light displays, creating a vibrant gathering spot for visitors and locals alike.

For a more local experience, head to Schönhauser Allee in Prenzlauer Berg, where smaller shops and cafes celebrate the season with creative decorations and festive displays.

Mitte is also not to be missed, especially around **Hackescher Markt,** where the charming courtyards are adorned with twinkling lights and decorations, providing a perfect backdrop for holiday shopping and socializing.

Photography Hotspots for Holiday Memories

Berlin's holiday lights and decorations create a dreamlike setting for capturing unforgettable memories.

For stunning holiday photos, begin at the Gendarmenmarkt, where the juxtaposition of the historical buildings and the festive lights provides a picturesque backdrop. The ambiance here is especially magical at dusk when the lights reflect off the cobblestones.

Another great spot is Charlottenburg Palace, where the grand architecture is beautifully illuminated against the evening sky.

The gardens are often decorated, creating a fairy-tale atmosphere perfect for romantic photos or family portraits. The Berlin Cathedral (Berliner Dom) is also a fantastic location, as its impressive facade becomes even more enchanting when lit up during the holiday season.

For unique shots, explore the Winterwald market in Görlitzer Park, where the combination of nature and festive decorations offers a more organic setting.

Capture candid moments as you stroll through the market, framed by the soft glow of lights and the laughter of families and friends enjoying the holiday spirit.

Remember to bring a camera or smartphone with ample battery and storage space—Berlin's holiday charm is sure to inspire a flurry of photos that you'll cherish for years to come.

Chapter 4: Cozy Cafés and Winter Treats

Warm Up with Berlin's Best Hot Drinks

As the temperatures drop in Berlin, nothing warms the soul quite like a steaming cup of a delicious hot drink. The city boasts an array of cozy cafés where you can escape the chill and indulge in seasonal beverages.

Begin your journey with a classic **Glühwein**, a spiced mulled wine traditionally served at Christmas markets. Many cafés and bars put their unique spin on this festive drink, so don't hesitate to try a few variations during your visit.

For a caffeine fix, head to one of Berlin's artisanal coffee shops, where expert baristas serve up rich, aromatic coffee blends.

Many of these cafés offer special holiday lattes infused with seasonal flavors like cinnamon, vanilla, and chestnut.

Try a Peppermint Hot Chocolate for a comforting twist, or indulge in a Chai Latte with a festive flair, featuring warming spices that evoke the spirit of the season.

Don't forget to seek out local favorites like Feuerzangenbowle, a theatrical drink made with rum-soaked sugar cones set on fire and poured over mulled wine.

This delightful concoction is not only delicious but also an unforgettable experience to share with friends and family in a cozy café setting.

Traditional Holiday Foods and Where to Find Them

Berlin's culinary scene comes alive during the holiday season, with traditional foods that reflect the city's rich culture and history.

One of the most beloved holiday treats is Stollen, a dense, fruit-filled bread dusted with powdered sugar.

This festive loaf can be found in bakeries throughout the city, but the Berliner Stollen at **Café Kranzler** is a local favorite and well worth a taste.

Another classic is the Currywurst, a staple of Berlin street food, especially popular during winter months. Head to Konnopke's Imbiss in Prenzlauer Berg to sample this iconic dish served with a generous drizzle of tangy curry ketchup.

For those with a sweet tooth, don't miss the Lebkuchen, spiced gingerbread cookies available at various Christmas markets and bakeries.

These delicious treats often come adorned with icing and festive decorations, making them perfect gifts or festive snacks.

Unique Seasonal Dishes and Delicacies

In addition to the holiday classics, Berlin's dining scene features unique seasonal dishes that highlight local ingredients and flavors.

Many restaurants embrace the winter season by offering hearty stews and roasts, perfect for warming up after a day of exploring the markets.

Seek out Rotkohl (red cabbage) and Kartoffelklöße (potato dumplings), popular accompaniments to winter meals that embody the comforting spirit of German cuisine.

For a truly memorable dining experience, consider reserving a table at a traditional German restaurant like Zur Letzten Instanz, where you can savor seasonal specialties such as Wildschweinbraten (wild boar roast) during the festive period.

Alternatively, modern eateries like Neni offer innovative twists on classic dishes, combining international flavors with local ingredients for a fresh take on holiday dining.

Don't forget to explore seasonal food stalls at the Christmas markets, where you'll find an array of unique offerings, from raclette (melted cheese served with potatoes) to bratkartoffeln (crispy fried potatoes).

With so many delectable options, Berlin's cozy cafés and festive foods create an inviting atmosphere that captures the warmth of the holiday season.

Chapter 5: Berlin's Holiday Events and Performances

Classical Concerts and Opera for the Season

During the holiday season, Berlin's rich cultural heritage comes alive through a series of classical concerts and operatic performances that enchant audiences.

The Berlin Philharmonic, one of the world's leading orchestras, offers a magical series of holiday concerts, featuring festive pieces that evoke the spirit of the season.

Attending a performance in their stunning concert hall is an experience in itself, as the music fills the air with warmth and joy, making it a perfect outing for both music aficionados and casual listeners.

The State Opera Unter den Linden also stages special holiday performances, including traditional operas and ballets that celebrate the season.

Tchaikovsky's "The Nutcracker" is a perennial favorite, bringing to life a whimsical world of dancing snowflakes and sugar plum fairies. With its lavish sets and enchanting score, this ballet captures the essence of the holidays and is a delightful way to introduce children to the magic of live performances.

For those who prefer a more intimate setting, numerous churches throughout Berlin host classical music concerts, showcasing local choirs and talented musicians.

The Berlin Cathedral (Berliner Dom) is particularly notable for its holiday concerts, where visitors can enjoy the beautiful acoustics of this historic site while listening to festive choral music, creating an unforgettable atmosphere.

Festive Plays, Choirs, and Street Performers

The holiday season in Berlin also features an array of theatrical productions and live performances that add to the festive ambiance. Many theaters stage traditional Christmas plays, offering both classic tales and modern interpretations that capture the spirit of the season.

The **Volksbühne and the Grips** Theater are renowned for their engaging productions, often tailored to family audiences, making them a great choice for an evening out.

Street performers add to the charm of Berlin's winter landscape, particularly around busy market areas like Alexanderplatz and Gendarmenmarkt.

Here, you'll find everything from jugglers to musicians playing festive tunes, creating a lively atmosphere that invites passersby to stop, listen, and enjoy.

The sound of carolers fills the air, adding a nostalgic touch to the holiday experience. You may even encounter local choirs performing traditional German Christmas carols, inviting everyone to join in the festive singing.

Another unique event is the annual "Festival of Lights", which usually occurs in early December, where various landmarks around Berlin are illuminated with stunning light displays and artistic projections.

The festival draws locals and tourists alike, creating a vibrant nighttime atmosphere as visitors stroll through the city, marveling at the creative installations.

Family-Friendly Events and Activities

Berlin is a family-friendly city, especially during the holiday season, offering a plethora of activities designed to engage children and create cherished memories.

Many Christmas markets feature dedicated areas for kids, where they can enjoy rides, workshops, and meet Santa Claus. The Winterwald market in Görlitzer Park often has puppet shows, craft stations, and other fun activities tailored to younger visitors.

For a unique experience, families can participate in holiday-themed workshops offered by various cultural institutions.

Museums like the Berlin Natural History Museum and the German Museum of Technology frequently host festive events, including crafting sessions and storytelling workshops that educate and entertain.

Outdoor ice skating is another favorite winter activity, with numerous rinks popping up around the city, including the picturesque rink at Alexanderplatz.

Here, families can skate together, enjoying the festive lights and sounds while warming up afterward with hot cocoa from nearby stalls.

Many theaters and performance venues, such as the Puppentheater (Puppet Theater), offer special holiday performances that captivate young audiences with enchanting storytelling and delightful puppetry.

These engaging shows are perfect for sparking children's imaginations and introducing them to the joys of live theater.

Berlin's holiday events and performances create a tapestry of cultural experiences that embody the spirit of the season.

From classical concerts and festive plays to family-friendly activities, there's something for everyone to enjoy, ensuring that your time in Berlin is filled with laughter, joy, and holiday cheer.

Chapter 6: Outdoor Winter Fun

Skating Rinks, Sledding Hills, and Ice Trails

When winter blankets Berlin in snow, the city transforms into a playground for outdoor enthusiasts.

One of the most popular winter activities is ice skating, and Berlin boasts numerous outdoor rinks that cater to all ages. The iconic Alexanderplatz rink is a favorite, located in the heart of the city with stunning views of the TV Tower.

Skating here surrounded by holiday lights creates a magical atmosphere, perfect for a family outing or a romantic evening.

For a more picturesque experience, head to the Ernst-Reuter-Platz, where the rink is set against the backdrop of beautiful historic buildings. Another hidden gem is the Tegeler See, a natural lake that becomes a fantastic ice skating destination when frozen.

You can glide across the ice while taking in the serene winter landscape.

For thrill-seekers, Berlin's sledding hills are a must-visit. Volkspark Friedrichshain offers several slopes that are perfect for sledding, with plenty of space for families to set up and enjoy a day of winter fun.

Tempelhofer Feld, the former airport turned park, also features gentle hills that are ideal for sledding and even kite flying on windy days. Be sure to bring your sled or rent one at local shops to maximize your outdoor enjoyment.

Additionally, ice trails are becoming increasingly popular in Berlin, offering unique paths for skaters to explore.

The Lichtenberg District features an enchanting trail winding through a scenic park, perfect for a leisurely skate amid nature. The combination of outdoor ice skating and beautiful winter scenery creates a captivating experience.

Berlin's Best Parks and Gardens in Winter

Berlin is home to numerous parks and gardens that take on a different charm in the winter months.

Tiergarten, the city's largest park, offers a serene winter landscape with its winding paths lined by snow-covered trees.

Stroll through the park to admire the picturesque sights, and stop by the Siegessäule (Victory Column) for breathtaking panoramic views of the city.

Another lovely spot is Schlossgarten Charlottenburg, where the palace grounds become a winter wonderland.

The beautifully landscaped gardens, blanketed in snow, create a romantic setting for leisurely walks or intimate picnics (albeit a chilly one).

The Botanical Garden is also worth visiting during winter, where you can explore the tranquil beauty of exotic plants and enjoy the unique experience of the lush conservatories against the cold outside.

For families, Volkspark Humboldthain features a children's playground that remains open during winter, along with expansive green spaces for snowball fights or building snowmen.

The park's elevated areas also provide excellent views of the surrounding cityscape, making it a great spot to take in the winter scenery.

How to Enjoy Berlin's Snowy Side

Experiencing Berlin's snowy side requires a spirit of adventure and a few essentials. First and foremost, dress warmly in layers to ensure comfort during your outdoor excursions.

Waterproof boots and insulated outerwear are essential for keeping warm and dry while exploring the winter landscape.

One of the best ways to enjoy the snow is by taking a walk through the city's quieter neighborhoods, where the snow-covered rooftops and tree-lined streets create a picturesque scene. Prenzlauer Berg is particularly charming, with its historic buildings and cozy cafés inviting you to take a break from the cold.

For a unique experience, consider renting a snow-covered bicycle or a sled to navigate the city in a fun and playful way.

Some parks even offer rental services for sleds, allowing you to experience the joy of gliding downhill without needing to invest in your own equipment.

Finally, don't forget to indulge in Berlin's seasonal culinary offerings as you explore. After a day of winter activities, warm up with a steaming cup of glühwein or hot chocolate at one of the many outdoor stalls near the skating rinks or parks. Treat yourself to a slice of Stollen or freshly baked Lebkuchen to complete the experience.

Berlin in winter is a vibrant blend of outdoor fun, picturesque parks, and charming festivities.

Whether you're ice skating, sledding, or simply taking in the snowy scenery, there's no shortage of ways to enjoy the city's winter charm. Embrace the cold, revel in the beauty, and create lasting memories during your winter adventure in Berlin.

Chapter 7: Shopping for Gifts and Souvenirs

Berlin's Unique Artisan Shops

When it comes to gift shopping in Berlin, the city offers a wealth of unique artisan shops that showcase the creativity and craftsmanship of local artisans.

One of the best areas to explore these hidden gems is Kreuzberg, known for its vibrant arts scene and eclectic shops. Here, you'll find everything from handmade jewelry to bespoke clothing.

Hallesches Haus is a must-visit, featuring a carefully curated selection of homewares, furniture, and locally sourced goods that reflect Berlin's contemporary design aesthetic.

Another hotspot for artisan shopping is the Mitte district, where you can discover Bergmannstraße, lined with charming boutiques and shops that offer a range of handcrafted items.

Mauerpark, famous for its flea market on Sundays, is an excellent place to hunt for unique vintage finds and artisanal goods. From handmade leather goods to locally crafted ceramics, you're sure to uncover one-of-a-kind treasures that make for perfect gifts.

Don't miss Mademoiselle D, a delightful shop specializing in vintage and handcrafted fashion pieces, or Manufaktur in Friedrichshain, where you can find exquisite textiles and decorative items made by local artisans.

Each purchase from these shops not only supports local craftsmen but also provides you with a distinctive piece of Berlin to take home.

Christmas Market Treasures to Bring Home

Berlin's Christmas markets are a treasure trove of unique gifts and souvenirs, each offering a delightful array of handmade products that embody the holiday spirit.

As you wander through the bustling stalls, be on the lookout for hand-carved wooden ornaments, which are often intricately designed and make for charming decorations to adorn your tree at home.

One of the highlights is the Gendarmenmarkt Christmas Market, renowned for its artisan crafts, including glass-blown ornaments and traditional nutcrackers. These high-quality, handcrafted items not only capture the essence of German Christmas traditions but also serve as beautiful keepsakes for years to come.

For those looking to take home a taste of Berlin, consider purchasing local delicacies like marzipan from the Charlottenburg Palace Christmas Market or artisanal chocolates from one of the many stalls.

Lebkuchen, or gingerbread cookies, often beautifully decorated and packaged, are also a popular choice. Pair these treats with a bottle of glühwein or a locally brewed craft beer, and you'll have a delightful gift that captures the flavors of the city.

Additionally, many markets feature stalls run by local NGOs or social enterprises, where proceeds support community projects. By shopping at these stalls, you not only find unique gifts but also contribute to meaningful causes, making your purchases all the more special.

Eco-Friendly and Local Shopping Tips

In recent years, there has been a growing emphasis on sustainable shopping practices in Berlin, and the holiday season is no exception.

When shopping for gifts and souvenirs, consider opting for eco-friendly products that reflect a commitment to sustainability. Many local shops prioritize sustainable materials and ethical production methods, making it easier to find gifts that align with environmentally conscious values.

Look for products made from recycled materials, such as upcycled fashion from local designers or eco-friendly home goods from shops like Kollwitzplatz. These gifts not only support local businesses but also help reduce environmental impact.

When exploring the Christmas markets, bring your own reusable shopping bag to minimize waste, and consider purchasing items in bulk to reduce packaging.

Many vendors are happy to accommodate sustainable practices, allowing you to enjoy the festive shopping experience while being mindful of your environmental footprint.

Another tip for eco-conscious shopping is to seek out local artisans who prioritize craftsmanship over mass production. By choosing handmade items, you not only support the local economy but also ensure that your gifts are unique and meaningful.

Finally, consider giving experiences instead of physical gifts. Many local businesses offer workshops, tours, and activities that provide a unique way to experience Berlin.

From cooking classes to guided city tours, gifting an experience allows your loved ones to create lasting memories while supporting local artisans and businesses.

In Berlin, shopping for gifts and souvenirs during the holiday season is an experience filled with creativity, sustainability, and local charm.

Whether you're exploring artisan shops, uncovering treasures at the Christmas markets, or opting for eco-friendly options, each purchase tells a story and connects you to the vibrant spirit of this remarkable city.

Chapter 8: Berlin's Historic Christmas Sites

Churches, Cathedrals, and Nativity Scenes

Berlin's rich history is beautifully showcased in its churches and cathedrals, many of which become focal points of holiday celebrations during the Christmas season.

One of the most iconic is the Berlin Cathedral (Berliner Dom), located on Museum Island. Its stunning dome and baroque architecture provide a majestic backdrop for Christmas services and concerts.

Visitors can admire the cathedral's elaborate nativity scene, which depicts the story of Jesus' birth in exquisite detail. The serene atmosphere inside the cathedral, enhanced by the sound of the organ playing Christmas hymns, makes it a perfect place for reflection and celebration.

Another historic gem is the St. Mary's Church (Sankt Marienkirche), one of the oldest churches in Berlin. Its beautiful Gothic architecture and peaceful ambiance attract visitors looking to experience a traditional holiday service.

The church typically hosts Christmas concerts featuring local choirs and musicians, adding to the festive spirit.

The nativity scene here is particularly enchanting, crafted by local artisans and surrounded by twinkling lights that create a warm, inviting atmosphere.

For a more contemporary experience, the Trinitatis Church in Kreuzberg features an impressive nativity installation that captures the essence of diversity in Berlin.

Each year, the church invites artists from various backgrounds to create a unique interpretation of the nativity scene, reflecting the multicultural fabric of the city.

Holiday Traditions in Berlin's Historic Districts

Berlin's historic districts are steeped in holiday traditions that bring the city to life during the Christmas season.

In Charlottenburg, the Christmas market outside the Charlottenburg Palace is a highlight, where visitors can wander through stalls selling traditional crafts, holiday foods, and warm beverages.

The palace itself is adorned with festive decorations, and the annual lighting of the Christmas tree is a must-see event that attracts both locals and tourists.

In the Nicholas Quarter (Nikolaiviertel), visitors can step back in time and experience a traditional Christmas as they stroll through its cobblestone streets.

This area is famous for its charming, historic buildings and quaint shops. Here, you can find unique holiday gifts and decorations, as well as delicious seasonal treats like roasted chestnuts and spiced cookies.

The annual Christmas market in Nikolaiviertel offers a cozy atmosphere, complete with live music and performances that showcase local talent.

The Gendarmenmarkt, one of the most beautiful squares in Berlin, hosts a renowned Christmas market where visitors can enjoy performances by local choirs and musicians amidst the backdrop of the stunning French Cathedral and German Cathedral.

This festive market is known for its handcrafted goods and gourmet food stalls, making it a perfect spot to soak in Berlin's holiday traditions.

Walking Tour Ideas for a Festive Day Out

Exploring Berlin's historic Christmas sites on foot is an excellent way to immerse yourself in the festive spirit.

Start your walking tour at Alexanderplatz, where you can enjoy the vibrant Christmas market before heading towards Nikolaiviertel. Along the way, be sure to stop at the Berlin Cathedral to marvel at its grandeur and the nativity scene inside.

After exploring Nikolaiviertel, continue your stroll to Gendarmenmarkt, taking in the architectural beauty of the surrounding buildings.

Enjoy a hot drink as you browse the market stalls and listen to live music. From there, make your way to the Charlottenburg Palace, where you can spend some time at the market before taking a leisurely walk through the palace gardens, which are beautifully illuminated for the holiday season.

For a unique twist, consider taking an evening walking tour that highlights Berlin's historic sites adorned with Christmas lights.

Many local companies offer guided tours that focus on the city's holiday traditions, complete with stories of the past and insights into how Berliners celebrate Christmas.

These tours often include stops at notable churches, historic landmarks, and lesser-known sites that are particularly enchanting during the winter months.

As you stroll through the historic districts, don't forget to capture the moments with your camera.

The juxtaposition of Berlin's rich history against the backdrop of festive decorations and twinkling lights creates countless photo opportunities that will help you remember your holiday experience in the city.

Berlin's historic Christmas sites offer a blend of tradition, culture, and holiday cheer. By exploring its churches, markets, and neighborhoods, you can immerse yourself in the festive spirit and create lasting memories of this vibrant city during the most wonderful time of the year.

Chapter 9: Berlin's Christmas for Kids

Family-Friendly Markets and Rides

Berlin comes alive with magic during the Christmas season, offering a plethora of family-friendly activities that make it an ideal destination for kids.

One of the highlights is the Christmas markets, many of which are specially designed with children in mind.

The Winterwelt at Potsdamer Platz is a must-visit, featuring an enchanting array of attractions. Here, children can glide across the ice rink, enjoy rides on the charming carousel, and take in the festive lights that transform the area into a winter wonderland.

The Gendarmenmarkt Christmas Market is another fantastic option for families. Not only can kids enjoy delicious treats like roasted chestnuts and gingerbread cookies, but they can also participate in craft workshops where they can create their own holiday decorations.

The market's festive atmosphere is further enhanced by street performers and live music, making it a delightful outing for the whole family.

For a more hands-on experience, the Spandau Christmas Market offers an array of family-friendly rides and attractions, including a Ferris wheel that provides breathtaking views of the festive surroundings.

The market's cozy setting allows families to wander through stalls selling handmade gifts while enjoying the holiday cheer.

Where to See Santa and Festive Parades

One of the most exciting aspects of Christmas in Berlin for children is the chance to meet Santa Claus. Various Christmas markets throughout the city host special visits from Santa, who is often found in his festive hut surrounded by twinkling lights and holiday decorations.

Kids can share their Christmas wishes, and many markets offer photo opportunities to capture these magical moments.

The Christmas Parade in Berlin is another highlight that families will not want to miss. Taking place in December, this festive event features colorful floats, cheerful music, and lively performances that celebrate the spirit of the season.

Children will love the vibrant atmosphere, filled with laughter and joy as they watch Santa and his helpers spread holiday cheer through the streets.

For a more intimate experience, consider visiting Winterwald, a magical forest experience in the heart of the city. Here, kids can participate in storytelling sessions, craft workshops, and interactive activities designed to immerse them in the Christmas spirit.

Top Activities and Events for Little Ones

Berlin offers a range of activities and events specifically tailored to younger visitors during the holiday season. The Berlin Zoo, one of the city's most beloved attractions, hosts a special Christmas program that includes festive decorations and themed activities.

Kids can enjoy holiday-themed animal encounters and participate in craft workshops that educate them about wildlife while celebrating the season.

Another popular destination is Legoland Discovery Centre in Potsdamer Platz, which hosts a winter wonderland event.

Children can enjoy building their own festive creations out of LEGO bricks, participate in themed activities, and explore the illuminated displays that celebrate the holiday season.

For those seeking interactive fun, Theater der Erfahrungen offers family-friendly Christmas performances featuring puppetry and engaging storytelling.

These performances often incorporate traditional German holiday tales, making them both entertaining and educational.

In addition to these activities, many libraries and community centers in Berlin host Christmas-themed storytelling sessions and craft workshops for children. These events are designed to foster creativity and provide families with a chance to engage in the holiday spirit together.

Berlin during Christmas is a magical experience for families, with an abundance of activities that cater to the interests and imaginations of children.

From festive markets filled with rides and crafts to opportunities to meet Santa and enjoy parades, the city ensures that the holiday season is filled with joy and laughter for kids of all ages.

As you explore Berlin's Christmas offerings, you'll create cherished memories that your family will treasure for years to come.

Chapter 10: Holiday Reflections: Berlin in a New Year Glow

New Year's Celebrations in Berlin

As the holiday season comes to a close, Berlin transforms into a vibrant hub of festivities, celebrating the arrival of the New Year with unparalleled enthusiasm. Known for its electrifying atmosphere, Berlin's New Year's Eve celebrations draw crowds from around the world.

One of the most iconic events is the New Year's Eve Party at the Brandenburg Gate, where revelers gather to welcome the New

Year amidst a spectacular fireworks display. The party features live music performances, DJ sets, and a festive ambiance that sets the tone for an unforgettable night.

In addition to the festivities at the Brandenburg Gate, various venues across the city host their own celebrations, ranging from intimate gatherings to grand parties.

Berlin's diverse nightlife ensures that there is something for everyone, whether you prefer an upscale gala or a laid-back pub atmosphere.

Many locals and tourists alike choose to bring their own champagne and snacks to enjoy as they watch the city light up with fireworks.

Places to Celebrate and Ring in the New Year

For those looking to celebrate New Year's Eve in style, Berlin boasts a plethora of venues that cater to different tastes. Fritz Club, located at the famous Friedrichshain club, is known for its pulsating music and vibrant atmosphere.

The club typically hosts a New Year's Eve party featuring top DJs and an impressive light show, making it a popular choice for partygoers.

If you prefer a more laid-back vibe, consider the Spreeufer River. Here, you can enjoy a scenic view of the fireworks over the water while sipping on a warm drink from one of the nearby stalls. Many people gather along the banks of the river, creating a relaxed yet festive atmosphere perfect for ringing in the New Year with friends and family.

For families or those seeking a unique experience, the Berlin TV Tower (Fernsehturm) offers a special New Year's Eve dining event. Guests can enjoy a gourmet meal while taking in panoramic views of the city's skyline.

As the clock strikes midnight, the tower provides a breathtaking vantage point to watch the fireworks illuminate the Berlin sky.

Post-Holiday Relaxation Spots

After the excitement of the New Year's celebrations, Berlin offers a wealth of options for post-holiday relaxation.

The city's parks and gardens, such as Tiergarten, are ideal for leisurely strolls and unwinding amidst nature. The crisp winter air and peaceful surroundings provide the perfect backdrop for reflecting on the year gone by and making plans for the future.

For those seeking a cozy retreat, many cafés and tea houses across the city create a warm, inviting atmosphere perfect for unwinding. Consider visiting Café Einstein, a historic coffee house known for its classic Viennese coffee and delectable pastries.

It's an ideal spot to relax and reflect while savoring a hot drink.

If you're looking for a more rejuvenating experience, indulge in a visit to one of Berlin's renowned spas. Vabali Spa, inspired by Balinese wellness traditions, offers a serene escape from the bustling city.

With its saunas, pools, and wellness treatments, it provides a tranquil environment to relax and rejuvenate after the festive whirlwind.

As the New Year unfolds, Berlin invites you to embrace a time of reflection and renewal. With its vibrant celebrations, diverse venues, and calming retreats, the city offers a unique blend of excitement and tranquility, making it the perfect destination to welcome a new beginning.

Whether you find yourself celebrating with fireworks or enjoying a quiet moment in a café, Berlin's New Year glow will leave you with cherished memories and a sense of hope for the year ahead.

Final Tips for a Memorable Berlin Christmas

Staying Safe and Comfortable in Winter

Visiting Berlin during the winter months can be an enchanting experience, but it's essential to stay safe and comfortable while enjoying the festivities. First and foremost, dressing in layers is crucial.

The weather can be quite cold, with temperatures often dipping below freezing. Start with a moisture-wicking base layer, add insulating layers like sweaters or fleeces, and top it off with a warm, waterproof coat.

Don't forget accessories such as a scarf, gloves, and a hat to keep you warm during your outdoor explorations.

When navigating the city, be cautious of icy sidewalks and streets, especially in the early mornings or after fresh snowfall.

Sturdy footwear with good traction is advisable. While Berlin is generally safe, it's always wise to remain aware of your surroundings, particularly in crowded areas like Christmas markets. Keep your belongings secure and avoid displaying valuable items openly.

Additionally, consider the city's public transport system, which is efficient and well-connected. Familiarize yourself with the U-Bahn and S-Bahn lines to easily navigate from one festive destination to another.

If you plan to enjoy the vibrant nightlife, opt for public transport or taxis rather than walking alone late at night.

Making the Most of Your Berlin Holiday Journey

To fully embrace the magic of Christmas in Berlin, it's essential to plan your itinerary wisely. Prioritize the Christmas markets, as each offers a unique experience, from traditional crafts to culinary delights.

Consider visiting both well-known markets like Gendarmenmarkt and hidden gems like the market in the Nikolaiviertel for a diverse experience.

Allocate time for cultural exploration as well. Berlin's rich history and vibrant art scene are not to be missed.

Take the opportunity to visit museums, galleries, and historic sites, and incorporate local traditions into your visit, such as attending a holiday concert or visiting a church for a festive service.

Engage with locals to learn about their holiday traditions, and don't hesitate to ask for recommendations on hidden spots or unique events happening during your visit. Embracing spontaneity can lead to unexpected adventures and deeper connections with the city.

Words of Farewell and Inspiration

As your journey through Berlin's Christmas landscape comes to a close, take a moment to reflect on the experiences and memories you've created.

The joy of the holiday season is amplified in a city that celebrates with such enthusiasm and warmth. Allow the festive spirit to inspire you as you return home, carrying with you the sights, sounds, and flavors of Berlin.

Consider keeping a travel journal or creating a photo book to document your experiences. Sharing your stories and memories with friends and family can keep the magic of Berlin alive long after the holiday lights have dimmed.

Remember that travel is not just about the destinations, but the connections we make and the lessons we learn along the way.

As you step into the new year, carry with you the inspiration drawn from Berlin's festive atmosphere, the kindness of its people, and the beauty of its traditions.

May these experiences encourage you to embrace adventure, seek new horizons, and continue exploring the world with an open heart and mind.

In the words of author Pico Iyer, "We travel, initially, to lose ourselves; and we travel, next, to find ourselves." Let your time in Berlin serve as both a joyous escape and a path toward deeper self-discovery as you celebrate the magic of the season and the beauty of life's journey.

Made in the USA
Monee, IL
11 November 2024

69781836R00059